Essential Life Science

PLANTS

Melanie Waldron

D1423536

520 971 83 X

Raintree is an imprint of Capstone Global Library Limited, a company incorporated in England and Wales having its registered office at 7 Pilgrim Street, London, EC4V 6LB – Registered company number: 6695582

www.raintreepublishers.co.uk
myorders@raintreepublishers.co.uk

Text © Capstone Global Library Limited 2014
First published in hardback in 2014
First published in paperback 2015
The moral rights of the proprietor have been asserted.

All rights reserved. No part of this publication may be reproduced in any form or by any means (including photocopying or storing it in any medium by electronic means and whether or not transiently or incidentally to some other use of this publication) without the written permission of the copyright owner, except in accordance with the provisions of the Copyright, Designs, and Patents Act 1988 or under the terms of a licence issued by the Copyright Licensing Agency, Saffron House, 6–10 Kirby Street, London EC1N 8TS (www.cla.co.uk). Applications for the copyright owner's written permission should be addressed to the publisher.

Edited by Andrew Farrow and Diyan Leake
Designed by Victoria Allen
Original illustrations © Capstone Global Library Ltd 2014
Picture research by Ruth Blair
Production by Sophia Argyris
Originated by Capstone Global Library Ltd
Printed in China by CTPS

ISBN 978 1 406 26231 5 (hardback)
17 16 15 14 13
10 9 8 7 6 5 4 3 2 1

ISBN 978 1 406 26241 4 (paperback)
18 17 16 15 14
10 9 8 7 6 5 4 3 2 1

British Library Cataloguing in Publication Data
Waldron, Melanie.
 Plants. -- (Essential life science)
 1. Plant physiology--Juvenile literature. 2. Plant ecology--Juvenile literature.
 I. Title II. Series
 580-dc23

Acknowledgements
We would like to thank the following for permission to reproduce photographs: Alamy pp. 10 (© Nigel Cattlin), 14 (© Emmanuel Lattes), 21 (© Tim Gainey), 25 (© Design Pics Inc.), 33 (© John Warburton-Lee Photography), 36 (© Corbis Cusp), 38 (© blickwinke), 41 (© blickwinkel), 43 (© MJ Photography); Capstone Publishers (© Karon Dubke) pp. 12,13, 18, 19, 30, 31; Corbis pp. 4 (© Luc Beziat/cultura), 40 (© Peggy Heard/Frank Lane Picture Agency); Getty Images pp. 5 (Dorling Kindersley), 9 (Village Production), 32 (Tareq Saifur Rahman), 35 (Ed Reschke); Shutterstock pp. 7 (© Ian Lee), 11 (©.Angela Waye), 16 (© FocalPoint), 22 (© Daniel Prudek), 23 (© Viktar Malyshchyts), 24 (© CreativeNature.nl), 26 (© Ferderic B), 27 (© Liu Jixing), 28 (© junjun), 37 (© Dirk Ercken), 39 (© Christopher Elwell), 42 (© szefei); Superstock p. 34 (Don Paulson Photography/Purestock).

Cover photograph of red and yellow tropical flower reproduced with permission of Corbis (© moodboard).

Every effort has been made to contact copyright holders of material reproduced in this book. Any omissions will be rectified in subsequent printings if notice is given to the publisher.

Disclaimer
All the internet addresses (URLs) given in this book were valid at the time of going to press. However, due to the dynamic nature of the internet, some addresses may have changed, or sites may have changed or ceased to exist since publication. While the author and publisher regret any inconvenience this may cause readers, no responsibility for any such changes can be accepted by either the author or the publisher.

Contents

Eureka moment!

Learn about important discoveries that have brought about further knowledge and understanding.

DID YOU KNOW?

Discover fascinating facts about plants.

WHAT'S NEXT?

Read about the latest research and advances in essential science.

Some words are shown in bold, **like this**. You can find out what they mean by looking in the glossary.

What would we do without plants?

Take a look outside. Wherever you are in the world, you will find plants growing. From the tallest trees to the tiniest flowers, plants cover the land. Sometimes they help to shape the landscape. For example, some huge sand dunes are held together by plants such as marram grass.

Plants feed us, and some can provide medicines for us. They provide food and homes for animals. Think of all the things made out of wood from trees! Some plants, such as cotton, are made into clothing.

DID YOU KNOW?

There are around 400,000 **species** of flowering plants in the world. Not all flowering plants have large, colourful flowers. For example, grass is a type of flowering plant. Scientists think that there are many more flowering plants still to be discovered.

Grass is a plant that grows well all around the world. We often use it like an outdoor carpet! It also feeds animals who graze on it.

Why are plants important?

Plants are very important, because they are at the bottom of **food chains**. Animals that eat plants are called **herbivores**. Many herbivores are eaten by animals that eat meat. Without plants, there would be no herbivores, and without herbivores, there would be no meat-eating animals.

There are many different colours and shapes of flowering plants in the world. Some have very large, colourful flowers.

Eureka moment!

Scientists have explored the world to find new species of plant. However, in 2009 scientists discovered a new one growing right under their noses in the Royal Botanic Gardens in Kew, London. An undiscovered plant had been growing in a greenhouse there for 50 years! It is a herb called *Isoglossa variegata*, and it comes from Africa.

What are plants?

Earth's living things can be sorted into five groups. Animals are one group, plants are another. You can usually tell plants from animals. Most plants stay in the same place, usually fixed to the ground. They don't have brains or **nerves** to send signals around their different parts. They can make food for themselves using sunlight, so they don't have to eat other things. Humans and other animals then use plants as food.

Animals - Most move around
- Eat other things

Plants - Don't move around
- Make food for themselves

Protists - Tiny living things
- Live in water

Fungi - Don't make food for themselves
- Grow in damp places

Bacteria - Tiny living things
- Live in air, soil, and water

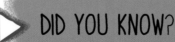

This diagram shows the five groups of living things on Earth, together with key features for each group.

DID YOU KNOW?

There is a group of living things that you might think of as plants, but which are not actually plants. The fungus group includes mushrooms and toadstools. They are not plants, because they do not use sunlight to make food for themselves.

Groups of plants

There are different groups of plants – flowering plants, conifers, ferns, liverworts, and mosses. Flowering plants, conifers, and ferns are all vascular plants. This means that they have little tubes inside them, to transport water and food around their parts. Liverworts and mosses are non-vascular plants They have no tubes, and usually live in damp places.

Flowering plants and conifers make new plants from seeds. Ferns, liverworts, and mosses make new plants from **spores**.

This is a fern leaf. Ferns do not grow flowers and make seeds. Instead, they have tiny spores on their leaves that can grow into new plants.

Plant parts

Many plants have very similar parts. The **stem** is the main part that grows from the ground. It supports the plant, and tubes inside the stem carry water and food. **Roots** are the parts that grow under the ground. They hold the plant in place, and soak up water and **nutrients** from the soil.

Along the stem, plants produce leaves. Leaves come in all sorts of shapes and sizes. They make food for the plant. Flowers are where the plant makes seeds that will grow into new plants.

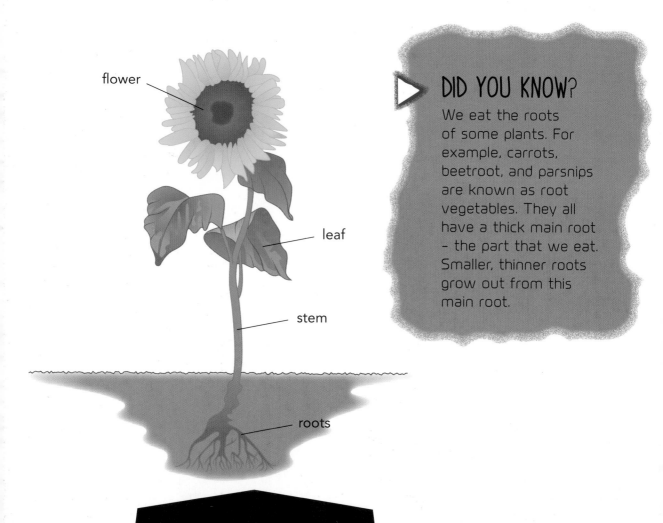

flower

leaf

stem

roots

DID YOU KNOW?

We eat the roots of some plants. For example, carrots, beetroot, and parsnips are known as root vegetables. They all have a thick main root – the part that we eat. Smaller, thinner roots grow out from this main root.

This diagram shows some of the parts that most flowering plants have.

Strong stems

Tall plants that live for a long time, such as trees, need to develop very strong, thick stems. They do this by growing new stem material near the centre. This pushes the older stem material out, so the stem gets thicker and thicker. Over time, this hardens into wood. A protective coating called bark forms on the outside.

Eureka moment!

In the early 1900s, A. E. Douglass developed a process called dendrochronology. This is studying the growth rings in tree trunks. Growth rings are caused when trees grow more at certain times of year – for example, in the summer. Scientists can count the rings to tell how old the tree is.

Some trees grow to enormous sizes, and need strong stems. We call tree stems trunks.

Inside plant parts

Have you ever seen something sticky oozing from a cut in a tree trunk? Or from the end of cut flower stems? This is called **sap**. Sap is a liquid inside plants that contains water and food for the plant. It is contained in the plant's **cells**. Cells are like tiny building blocks that make up all parts of the plant.

▷ **DID YOU KNOW?**

Plants wilt, or droop over, when they don't have enough water inside their cells. The cells become soft and floppy, like a deflating balloon. When the plant gets watered, the cells take in water. This makes them tight and strong, like a fully blown balloon.

You can see this houseplant wilting after a time without water. Its cells are becoming soft and floppy.

Food and water tubes

All parts of a plant need food and water. They move around the plant inside tiny tubes. Most of the plant's water comes from the soil. The roots take in water and it travels up xylem tubes. These run up the stem and into the leaves. Food made in the leaves travels in phloem tubes to all parts of the plant.

▷ DID YOU KNOW?

Maple syrup is made from sap from sugar maple trees. The tree trunk is cut and the sap flows out into a collection pot. It is not good to eat straight away. First it needs to be boiled for a long time. This makes most of the water in it boil off, leaving behind the sweet, golden-brown syrup.

Tulip stems contain xylem and phloem tubes. The stem is covered by a thin layer called an epidermis, which is like skin for the plant.

Try this!

Vascular tubes in plants are essential for moving water and chemicals around the plant.

Prediction

White flowers cut and placed in a jar of coloured water will change colour as the water is transported in vascular tubes around the plants.

What you need

- two bunches of white flowers, such as carnations
- two vases large enough to hold the flowers
- water
- food colouring
- scissors

What you do

Make sure you handle the food colouring carefully so you don't stain your clothes!

(1) Using the scissors, cut the stems of the flowers carefully, about 5 centimetres (2 inches) from the bottom.

(2) Fill one vase almost full with water, and mix the food colouring into the water. Fill the other vase with water only.

3 Place a bunch of flowers into each vase. Leave them for a few days.

4 After a few days, look at the flowers. What colour are the petals of the flowers in the coloured water? What colour are the other flowers?

Conclusion
The flowers have turned the colour of the food colouring because their vascular tubes have transported the coloured water around them. The flowers in the clear water have remained white.

What do plants need to grow?

Plants need energy to grow. They get this energy from food that they make for themselves, in a process called **photosynthesis**. Photosynthesis mostly happens in the leaves of a plant. The leaves trap the sunlight using a green chemical called **chlorophyll**.

A plant needs water and sunlight for photosynthesis. It also needs a gas from the air called **carbon dioxide**, or CO_2. With these ingredients, the plant can produce sugary substances, which give the plant energy to grow.

DID YOU KNOW?

In autumn, trees stop making new chlorophyll. The old chlorophyll in the leaves breaks down. This makes the leaves change to lots of different and beautiful colours, including yellow, red, orange, and brown.

Chlorophyll is what makes leaves look green. Some plants have leaves that are not green. They still have chlorophyll, but they have other chemicals that hide the green colour.

Making oxygen

When photosynthesis happens, the plant produces food for itself and also a gas called oxygen. It releases some of this oxygen into the air. This is another reason why plants are so important to us – we need to breathe oxygen to keep us alive.

This diagram shows the process of photosynthesis. The blue arrows show what the plant needs for photosynthesis. The red arrows show what is produced from photosynthesis.

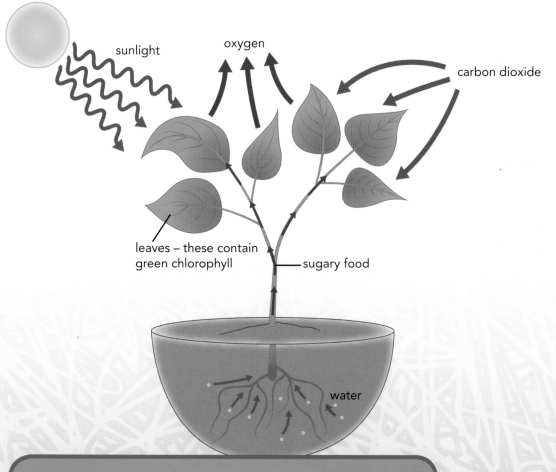

sunlight

oxygen

carbon dioxide

leaves – these contain green chlorophyll

sugary food

water

WHAT'S NEXT?

In 2011, a scientist spent 48 hours inside a sealed chamber that allowed no air into it. He did not suffocate, though, because also in the chamber were over 150 plants. They produced enough oxygen for the scientist to breathe in and stay alive.

Releasing energy

When plants have made food for themselves through photosynthesis, they can use this food to give them energy to grow. To get the energy from the food, they need oxygen. Plants use up a lot less oxygen than they make through photosynthesis. Using oxygen to release energy is called respiration. The oxygen you breathe is used in your body for respiration.

A seedling emerges and produces leaves which catch light to produce food and enable the plant to grow bigger.

Moving nutrients

You need chemicals called nutrients in your diet, to keep you healthy. Plants also need nutrients to help them grow and stay healthy. They get nutrients such as nitrogen and potassium from soil. These dissolve into water in the soil, and the plant can soak them up with the water, through its roots.

The plant moves water and nutrients through its parts by a process called transpiration. The plant loses water through tiny holes on its leaves called **stomata**. This makes more water move towards the stomata, to replace the water lost there. As the water moves up the plant, more water and nutrients are drawn into the plant by the roots.

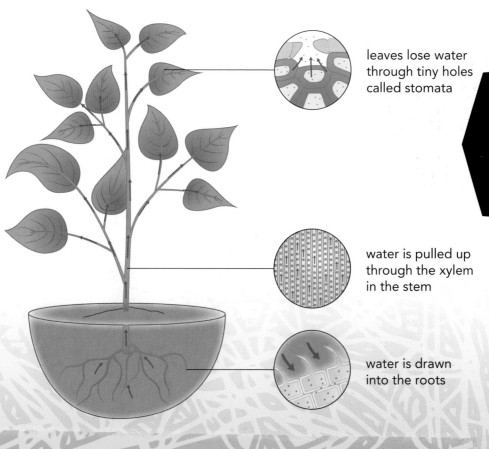

leaves lose water through tiny holes called stomata

This diagram shows how water moves through a plant.

water is pulled up through the xylem in the stem

water is drawn into the roots

Eureka moment!

In 1699, an English scientist called John Woodward tested different kinds of water on mint plants. The plant watered with rainfall – the purest water – grew the least. The plant watered with drain water from a nearby park, which had leaf mould added to it, grew the best. From this experiment, Wood worked out that plants need certain chemicals to grow well. We now know that these chemicals are nutrients.

Try this!

Plants need light, water, air, nutrients, and space to grow. In this experiment, you will see how limiting the amount of light, air, and water affects plants.

Prediction
A seedling with the correct amount of light, air, and water will grow better and look healthier than seedlings deprived of these things.

What you need:
- four plant seedlings
- a cardboard box
- large clear plastic tub with lid
- water in a jug

What you do

1. Place your four seedlings in their pots on a table, ideally outside, or below a window inside.

2. Place the cardboard box over the top of one seedling. This will limit the amount of light this seedling receives.

3 Place the next seedling inside the clear plastic tub, and tightly seal the lid of the tub. This seedling will have access to less fresh air than the other seedlings.

4 The last two seedlings can remain on the table, but mark one with a cross. You will not give this one any water.

5 Over the next week or two, give all the seedlings some water if their soil looks a bit dry, except the one marked with a cross.

6 After a couple of weeks, look at the seedlings. Which one has grown the most and looks healthiest? Which one has grown the least? Which one looks the least healthy?

Conclusion

The seedling with access to as much light, air, and water as it needs will grow better and be healthier than seedlings that have had these things limited.

How do plants make seeds and grow?

Like all living things, plants try to reproduce – make new plants. To do this, most plants need a male cell to join with a female cell. In flowering plants, male and female cells join to make seeds that can then grow into new plants.

Both male and female cells are found in plant flowers. The plant makes flowers in order to make seeds. The male cell is carried in **pollen** on the anther. It needs to join with the female cell, which is in the **ovule**. To do this, first the pollen needs to land on a part of the flower called the **stigma**. The male cell then travels down a tiny tube into the **ovary**, where the ovule is. Once the male and female cells have joined up, they become a seed. When a plant has made enough seeds, it no longer needs its flowers, so they wither and die.

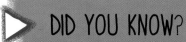

DID YOU KNOW?

Many flowers, such as tulips, have both male and female parts. Some plants, such as beech trees, produce male flowers and female flowers. A few plants, for example holly, produce only male or female flowers.

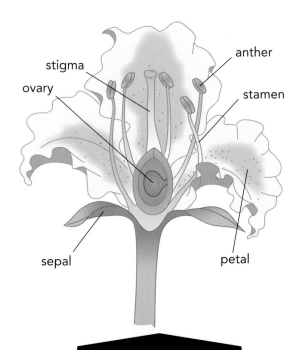

stigma

ovary

anther

stamen

sepal

petal

This flower has both male and female parts.

Pollination

Pollination is when pollen lands on stigmas. Pollen can be carried from flower to flower by the wind, or by animals. Flowers pollinated by the wind usually produce huge amounts of light pollen, which can be blown easily. The **stamens** and the stigmas often stick out beyond the flower petals, to increase the chance of pollen being blown off the stamens and on to the stigmas.

Some trees have tiny flowers that grow on long catkins, such as the male flowers on this hazel tree.

Pollination by animals

Many flowers are designed to attract insects, birds, and bats to them. They use bright colours and scent to do this. Lots of flowers also produce **nectar** for animals to eat, and they help the animals find the nectar by having "nectar guides". These are patterns on the petals that lead the animals to the nectar. As the animals enter the flowers, grains of pollen stick to them. When the animals enter different flowers, the pollen rubs on to the stigma, and pollination happens.

Some plants can pollinate themselves, when the stamen carrying the pollen bends over and touches the stigma.

The pollen from this yellow flower is sticking to the bee's legs and body. When the bee lands on another flower, the pollen can rub off on to the stigma.

Producing seeds

Once the male cell in pollen has joined with the female cell in the ovule, seeds can grow. They grow inside the female part of the plant called the ovary. The ovary changes to become a fruit, and seeds grow inside the fruit, protected by it.

Fruits can be juicy, like lemons, plums, and blackberries. They can be dry, like walnuts and acorns. They can have papery wings, like sycamore seed cases. They can also be pods, like pea pods.

Eureka moment!

In 2011, scientists discovered an orchid in south-east Asia that opens its flowers at night and closes them in the morning. They think it does this because it is pollinated by tiny flying insects, called midges, that are active at night.

Papayas are delicious, juicy fruits, full of little seeds.

DID YOU KNOW?

Conifer trees make seeds, but they don't produce fruits. The seeds are contained in cones. When the seeds are ready, the cones open and the seeds flutter out.

Scattering seeds

Once a plant's seeds are ready to grow into new plants, they need to be carried away from the plant to grow in a new space. This is so they don't use up any of the things that the parent plant needs, such as light, water, and nutrients. Plants have developed several different ways for this to happen.

Plants that make juicy, sweet fruits rely on animals to scatter their seeds. The animals eat the fruit, but the seeds pass straight through them and come out in their droppings. Some animals store seeds. For example, squirrels store acorns. If the acorns are stored in the right place, and the squirrel forgets about them, they can grow where they are hidden.

Some plant seeds, such as burdock seeds, hitch rides on animals. Their fruit cases have little hooks that catch on animals' fur. They can travel far like this, before dropping off on to the ground.

This wood mouse is eating a blackberry. The tiny seeds will pass through it and come out in its droppings.

Wind and water

Some fruits are very light and can be blown to new spaces by the wind. Dandelion fruits have "parachutes" to help the wind carry them far away. The parachutes are made of lots of tiny hairs.

Some fruits have a waterproof case and can float on water. Coconuts contain the seeds of coconut palm trees, which grow right next to the sea. The sea can carry coconuts huge distances, across oceans.

DID YOU KNOW?

Some plants have fruit pods that simply explode open when they are ready, or when they are touched by something such as raindrops or animals passing by. Himalayan balsam plants can shoot their seeds 7 metres (23 feet)!

This is a milkweed seed pod exploding. The seeds fly out, away from the parent plant.

Growing into new plants

Once seeds have left the plant and have landed on the ground, they can start to grow into new plants. This is called **germination**. To germinate, they need water, oxygen, and warmth.

If the conditions are right, the seeds **absorb** water from the ground. Inside the seed, a tiny root and a tiny **shoot** begin to grow. As these get bigger, they crack the seed's shell. The root pushes down into the soil, then the shoot pushes up to become the plant's stem. The stem grows one or two little seedling leaves. Once it grows its first true leaves – leaves that look like the parent plant's – it has finished germinating and can grow into a new plant.

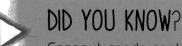

DID YOU KNOW?

Coconut seeds contain lots of food and water for the plant to use after it has germinated. This is useful because many coconuts wash up on beaches, where there is very little fresh water and few nutrients in the sand.

New plants without seeds

Some plants can grow new plants without using seeds. Strawberry plants send out long side shoots called runners. When the runners touch the soil, they start to grow roots and can grow into new plants. Once they have grown enough, the runner rots away.

Some plants, such as daffodils, can make bulbs. Bulbs are short, thick parts of the stem that are under ground. When the plant dies over winter, the bulbs stay alive and produce new plants the next year.

You can also grow some new plants by cutting a piece off. If you plant a rose cutting in soil, it will grow into a new rose bush.

What is a plant's life cycle?

Like animals, plants grow, make new plants, and then die. However, different types of plants have different life cycles. Annuals are plants that grow from a seed, make flowers and seeds, then die – all within a year. Biennials live for two years. In the first year, they grow leaves; in the second year, they make flowers and seeds before they die.

Perennial plants live for two or more years. They produce flowers and seeds every year. Trees are perennial plants. Some perennial plants look like they die every year, but the roots stay alive and the plant grows back the next year.

Peonies are perennial plants. Every year, they grow from their roots to produce masses of leaves and colourful flowers.

Plants and seasons

Countries that have warm summers and cool winters, like those in north-west Europe, have plants that are affected by the **seasons**. In spring, seeds start to germinate, and biennials and perennials start growing again. In summer, plants make flowers and seeds.

In autumn, fruits ripen and plants release their seeds. Tree leaves stop making new green chlorophyll. In winter, broad-leaved trees shed their leaves and live on food stored in their roots.

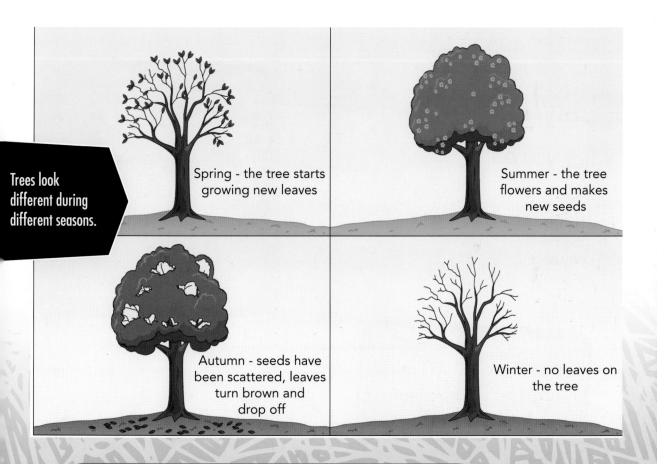

Trees look different during different seasons.

Spring - the tree starts growing new leaves

Summer - the tree flowers and makes new seeds

Autumn - seeds have been scattered, leaves turn brown and drop off

Winter - no leaves on the tree

WHAT'S NEXT?

Climate change may be changing the growth cycles of some plants. A study in the United Kingdom has shown that fruit trees are ripening around 18 days earlier than in the past. This may be good news for people, but it could have a bad impact on animals over the winter, as the fruit will be gone earlier.

Try this!

Seeds need warmth, oxygen, and water to germinate. This experiment will show the importance of warmth and water for germination.

Prediction
Dry seeds will not germinate, and a seed in a dark, cold, damp environment will germinate less quickly than a seed in a warm, damp environment.

What you need
- four bean seeds
- four cotton wool balls
- four plastic cups
- water

What you do

1. Place the four cotton wool balls into the bottom of the plastic cups, spread out to cover the bottom. Place one bean seed in each cup, on top of the cotton wool.

2. Mark two cups with a cross – you will not give any water to these seeds. Pour a little water into the other two cups, just enough to let the cotton wool soak it up.

3 Place one dry cup and one wet cup on a sunny windowsill, and one dry cup and one wet cup in a fridge.

4 Check on your seeds every day. Give the unmarked cups a little water if the cotton wool seems a bit dry. Do not water the marked cups.

5 After two or three days, look closely at your seeds. Record which seeds are sprouting first and growing quickest.

6 After a week or so, compare how well each seed has germinated. What has this shown you about what the seeds need to germinate?

Conclusion

The dry seeds have not germinated, showing that seeds need water to germinate. The wet seed in the fridge has germinated less than the wet seed on the windowsill, showing that seeds need warmth and light to germinate.

What adaptations do plants have?

Lots of plants have special **adaptations** to help them grow. These adaptations can help them cope with conditions such as cold climates or a lack of water.

Growing in water

Red mangroves are trees that grow in coastal areas. To help them stay upright in the soft, muddy soil, they grow lots of prop roots. These grow out from the stem and then down into the soil. They have lots of tiny holes on the surface so the plant can take in carbon dioxide when the lower roots are covered in water.

Some plants growing in rivers and lakes, such as water lilies, have leaves that float on the surface. Others, such as bulrushes, have leaves that stick above the surface. This helps them to capture sunlight and make food.

Water hyacinths float freely on the surface, with their roots hanging in the water. This means they can cover a huge area of water.

Coping with the cold

Some plants in cold environments have chemicals in their cells that stop them freezing solid. Plants in cold, windy places grow low on the ground to avoid the winds, and they have thick, waxy leaves to stop the wind from drying them out. On Mount Kenya in Africa, the giant lobelia has hairy stems and leaves to keep the plant warm. The giant groundsel has a thick layer of dead leaves on its stem. These help to protect the plant from freezing night-time temperatures.

These giant groundsels are growing on Mount Baker in Uganda in Africa.

DID YOU KNOW?

The reason that deciduous trees lose their leaves in winter is because the roots can't take in water if the ground is frozen. Their leaves would continue to lose water and the trees would suffer from drought if they did not shed their leaves.

Desert plants

In the world's hot deserts, the main problem for plants is the lack of water. Plants have adapted various ways of coping with this. Lots of desert plants have roots close to the ground. This means they can soak up rainwater quickly.

Many cactus plants, like this saguaro cactus, have pleats all around them. These can expand quickly to allow the plant to soak up as much water as possible in a rainstorm.

DID YOU KNOW?

A plant called *Agave franzosinii*, found in Mexican deserts, can take over 40 years to come into flower! It then grows a huge flower spike, around 10 metres (33 feet) tall. This produces lots of yellow flowers. Once it has flowered and made seeds, the plant then dies.

Cactus plants have thick stems that can store water for the plant. Very few have leaves, so the plant does not lose too much water. Instead, they have sharp spines, which help to stop animals from eating them. The thick stems contain the chlorophyll that the plants need for photosynthesis.

Climbing high

Some plants, such as sweet peas, grow quickly upwards before their stems are thick enough to support their weight. They have adapted to be able to do this by having tendrils. These are parts of leaves or stems that are like thin threads that can twist around things that they touch. By doing this, they can support the plant and allow it to grow taller than it could if it was just supported by its stem.

The tendrils on this American vetch plant are winding around a fence, supporting the plant.

Wet and dry seasons

In some areas of the world, the climate is hot and dry for much of the year, but in the rainy seasons it gets very wet. Grasses grow well in these areas. Their stems grow along the ground, and their side shoots grow upwards from the stems. In the hot, dry seasons, the grasses die back, waiting for rain. When the rainy seasons come, the grasses grow tall and green.

Wildebeest graze on the grasslands in Africa. The grasses can survive this grazing because the plants grow new shoots from the ground, where the stem is.

Rainforest plants

Plants grow well in warm, wet areas such as tropical rainforests. But because so many plants grow well, they shade out new plants trying to grow. Often, new plants can only grow when an old plant dies and falls, letting light into the forest floor. Some plants make seeds with huge stores of food for the seedlings so that they can grow quicker than other seedlings and reach up to the light first. Other rainforest plants have huge leaves, to capture as much light as possible.

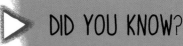

DID YOU KNOW?

A rainforest vine in Cuba attracts bats to pollinate it. It has disc-shaped leaves near its flowers. These discs bounce the bats' signals back, so the bat "hears" the plant and knows to go there for nectar!

Some rainforest trees produce flowers straight from their trunks, instead of high up on their branches. This is so that the animals that pollinate them can easily see and find the flowers.

Can plants defend themselves and attack others?

Many plants are good sources of food for herbivores. Plants can't move away or hide from these animals, so many have adapted ways of defending themselves. Other plants even eat animals!

Stings and thorns

Plants such as stinging nettles have tiny hairs on their leaves and stems. When something touches the plant, these hairs get broken, and a stinging chemical oozes out. Many animals avoid eating nettles because of the pain this chemical causes.

Some plants, such as roses and hawthorn trees, have sharp thorns along their stems and shoots. These make it difficult for animals to eat them.

Even lightly brushing past a nettle leaf will break the tiny hairs, releasing the stinging chemical on to your skin.

Don't eat me!

Some plants simply taste bad to herbivores, so animals learn to avoid these plants and find better-tasting ones instead. Bracken goes one step further. When animals chew the plant, the leaves release a powerful poison that can make animals very ill, and can even cause blindness.

Some plants use water to put off animals. Teasel plants have leaves that surround the stem. Water can collect here, forming little moats of water around the stem. This makes it impossible for some animals, such as snails and insects, to climb the stem and munch on the leaves above the moat.

DID YOU KNOW?

Some common garden plants are very poisonous. Foxgloves and oleander, for example, could make you sick and could even affect your heart if you ate them. Other plants, such as poison ivy, can harm your skin. Simply brushing by the plant and getting some sap on your skin can cause it to become sore and blistered.

Sheep do not like eating bracken. It is left to grow tall, while the sheep munch on the grass around it.

Camouflage and trickery

A few plants use **camouflage** as a way of avoiding being eaten by herbivores. Living stone plants grow among stones in desert areas. They store water in their odd-looking leaves, and much of the plant grows under the ground. They look very like stones, and so animals have trouble finding them.

Some passion flower vines have little egg-shaped tips on their leaves. This stops butterflies from laying their eggs on the leaves, as they want their eggs to hatch away from other eggs. Since the caterpillars that hatch from the eggs will eat leaves, the passion flower vine protects itself from being eaten.

This is a living stone plant. Can you tell it from the real stones next to it?